I0157815

From Death to Life, God's Path Toward a Resurrected Marriage

By Sharon V. Migala

Copyright © 2016 Sweet Psalm Publishing

Cover design copyright by Keith Alderman

Author photograph copyright by Carlia Alderman

Scripture quotations are taken from the Holy Bible, New Living Translation, copyright ©1996, 2004, 2007, 2013, 2015 by Tyndale House Foundation. Used by permission of Tyndale House Publishers, Inc., Carol Stream, Illinois 60188. All rights reserved.

Scripture quotations designated NIV are from THE HOLY BIBLE: NEW INTERNATIONAL VERSION. Copyright © 1973, 1978, 1984 by International Bible Society. All rights are reserved by Zondervan Publishing House.

Scripture quotations marked GWT are taken from the Holy Bible, GOD'S WORD®, © 1995 God's Word to the Nations. Used by permission of Baker Publishing Group

Scripture quotations marked NASB are taken from the New American Standard Bible, copyright © 1960, 1962, 1963, 1968, 1971, 1972, 1973, 1975, 1995 by The Lockman Foundation. Used by permission.

Scripture quotations from THE MESSAGE. Copyright © by Eugene H. Peterson 1993, 1994, 1995, 1996, 2000, 2001, 2002. Used by permission of NavPress. All rights reserved. Represented by Tyndale House Publishers, Inc.

All rights reserved.

The names and identifying details of many of the women and families whose stories appear in this book have been changed to protect their privacy.

ISBN-10:0692711112
ISBN-13:978-0692711118

DEDICATION

This book is for every heart that ever said, "Help, my marriage is drowning! I don't know what to do…."

God's Path Toward a Resurrected Marriage

CONTENTS

God's Path Toward a Resurrected Marriage

ACKNOWLEDGMENTS

All my heart to my husband Neil. You are a wonderful husband, amazing dad and great provider. The Lord has created you to leave a lasting impact on the world for Him. Thank you Neil for having a willing heart to follow where God was and is leading you.

Thank you to my awesome developmental editor Esther. You still amaze me how quickly you could get through a chapter. I am so thankful God picked you to join me on this journey.

To the brave ladies that shared their testimony, Janice, Carlia, Karen, Crystal, Tania, and Rebecca you are all warrior brides, thank you for choosing the path less traveled.

To all my good friends that helped with editing and encouraged me to keep going, Carlia, Jessica, Rebecca and Sarah, my cup overflows.

Keith, I so appreciate your time and graphic skills. Thank you for all your blood, sweat and tears to get the look I was after.

Thank you to my launch team, you have the power to alter someone's life by getting the word out that God can resurrect their marriage. Thank you for stepping up to the challenge.

Foundational Information

In order to get the most out of this book, there are certain foundational thoughts or actions that you will need to know or take, in order to receive the blessings the Lord has to give you. This foundation is what we will use to build upon in your journey to a resurrected marriage.

1. The most important foundational action is to be saved. I have written this book with the assumption that you have chosen to follow Jesus as your Lord and Savior. You can't operate in His power if you don't acknowledge that you choose Him to guide your life.

   John 3:16 (NLT) says, "For this is how God loved the world: He gave His one and only Son, so that everyone who believes in Him will not perish but have eternal life."

   If you haven't already chosen Jesus as your Lord and Savior and would like to, it is simple to start down this path. Tell Jesus you are sorry for your sins, you would like to receive the forgiveness He provided for when He died on the cross and you want Him to be your Lord and Savior. The exact words you use aren't as important as being heartfelt in choosing Him.

2. God is triune or a Trinity. He is God the Father, God the Son, and God the Holy Spirit. Each are God, and each hold unique attributes of Deity. The Bible contains many scriptures from Genesis, to Revelation revealing this amazing aspect of our God. I will not be doing a study on how to understand this as that would be a book in itself. Just know that I use the words God, Jesus and

Holy Spirit interchangeably depending on the attribute I want to highlight about the one True God.

3. When I mention the presence of God, I am speaking about a close personal encounter with Him. It can be a connection to one of our physical senses, or our spiritual senses. There are no specific ways it has to occur. It is about connecting one-on-one with the Creator of the Universe.

1

God is Powerful

I knew we had problems long before my husband, Neil, told me he wanted a divorce. We fought all the time. Vacations weren't fun; they were stressful. Life had become more about what I wanted instead of considering his needs, and it was apparent that Neil was just as intent on getting what he wanted as I was. But years of doing my own thing started catching up with me. Yes, I had often gone to church and read many part of the Bible, but I had no true understanding of what a relationship with God really was. That all changed, however, the day I felt a tug on my heart. It was a pull, as if someone was calling out to me to come close to them.

I was invited to start attending a local Bible study by my sister's mother-in-law. I felt drawn to go, and as each week came around, I became excited to be a part of it. The people were very welcoming, and I had a real sense that they wanted me there; which made it a lot easier to open up to them, especially considering where the state of my marriage was. As I spent more time in the Word, the Holy

Spirit began to gently convict me that I hadn't been the kind of wife He created me to be. I wanted, actually longed, to be a good wife, I just didn't know how. I needed to learn how to love through God's power and His perspective.

So this is where I was when Neil told me he wanted a divorce and that he never loved me. I was devastated. I cried and cried. I cried to God. I didn't know what to do. About that same time, my sister, Susan, told me that she had a friend whose marriage was restored by God. She gave me her email address and said I should think about contacting her; that she may be able to help me with my marriage.

Before Neil used the "D" word, I would have considered the help, but I believed the lie that divorce was the one word that would make my situation hopeless. So, I put the email address away and just lived life, as if on autopilot. I had no joy, no drive, and no hope that things could change. I continued to attend the Bible study and church, but how would I survive this?

Then one day, a tiny bit of hope arose and I decided to email her. The Holy Spirit was always speaking the truth, that He could bring about a healed marriage, but I had no vision for it. I explained to her that I didn't think there was any hope, as Neil was set on divorce. What could I, or she, or even God do? She wrote me a few things, but it was the power in one particular statement that changed my perspective; a statement that is as alive in me today, as it was the day I first read it.

"If Jesus raised Lazarus from the dead, He can resurrect your marriage."

POW! Right in the kisser! God had just become bigger in my mind. I hadn't realized how small I had made Him. Sure, God made the world, all the people, sent His Son to die and resurrect from the grave, but I was so disconnected from His power. How could His power affect my own life? This was a stake-in-the-ground moment for me in believing that our marriage could be restored. God sent a truth to me and I received it. God is so big and so powerful, and if I let Him, His power could change my life.

This book is about God's power and your heart. Let the truth of God's Word become your truth. You may feel like you are not loved. You may feel like you are in a hopeless situation. But those are just feelings. God's Word contains the power to change your life. Each chapter includes scripture verses that will point you to biblical truths you can grab hold of. I've included testimonies as a way to encourage your faith and to help you believe that you can have hope when all hope seems lost. And lastly, I have provided practical ways to help you in this journey. God's written word is POWERFUL and has the ability to change you!

My prayer is that you will let me impart hope into your situation. Each journey is unique and special, just as you are. May this book give you exactly what you need, to either bring you to, or keep you on the path the Lord has for you.

John 11:40-44 (NLT)
Jesus responded, "Didn't I tell you that you would see God's glory if you believe?" So they rolled the stone aside. Then Jesus looked up to heaven and said, "Father, thank you for hearing me. You always hear me, but I said it out loud for the sake of all these people standing here, so that they will believe you sent me." Then Jesus shouted, "Lazarus, come out!" And the dead man came out, his hands and feet bound in graveclothes, his face wrapped in a headcloth. Jesus told them, "Unwrap him and let him go!"

Be Encouraged

(Testimony by Janice)

Bruce and I had just celebrated our 15th wedding anniversary with what was supposed to be a beautiful trip to Jamaica. The trip turned out to be strained and filled with stressful, uncomfortable situations. Before we left, our marriage had been falling apart to say the least. Bruce had started a new job and was spending long hours in the office and staying out late at night with "clients". Money was flowing in, but the love in our marriage was flowing out.

When we returned from our trip, things deteriorated quickly. We had horrible fights and we were both miserable. One day, I asked Bruce if he loved me anymore. His answer was, "No, I don't believe I do love you anymore." I was devastated. He also suggested we separate for a while. I agreed, not knowing how to make someone love me again. The separation lasted almost two years, which included us getting a divorce.

After our divorce I ran into a friend, a Christian woman, and when she asked how I was doing, I began to sob and told her I was divorced. From that day forward, my life began to transform. I met with my friend weekly for hope, truth and encouragement, and went to Bible studies. I prayed and accepted Jesus as my Savior. My friend led me to God in a way I had never experienced before. My eyes were opened, and my life went through a transformation. I began to experience forgiveness, first of myself, then Bruce. All the anger and hurt began to melt away. I felt peace and joy in my heart, and then love for my husband.

Some days were difficult, but God's love kept me moving forward. During this time, Bruce was also saved. We met up one day and started talking. We realized that through forming a relationship with Jesus, we both had chosen to love each other again. We began going to church together and seeking God's Word as a couple. We remarried each other a few months later. We both know that through God's love, we have a renewed love and respect for one another.

Walk In It

When trials come, we each need to know we aren't alone, or the lies of hopelessness can creep in. Finding other people that have had their marriage restored through Jesus can be super encouraging. I encourage you to pray for God to bring you in contact with a variety of God-healed marriages. There are also lots of testimonies to be found online. I recommend checking out www.rejoiceministries.org, and going to their Saturday testimonies. God moves daily, and healed marriages are happening every day!

Power

Hebrews 4:12 (NLT)

For the word of God is alive and powerful. It is sharper than the sharpest two-edged sword, cutting between soul and spirit, between joint and marrow. It exposes our innermost thoughts and desires.

Some Things to Think About

1. What does a joy-filled life look like to you? On a scale from 1 to 10, what is your joy level?

_____

_____

_____

_____

_____

_____

_____

_____

_____

2. What we think about has the power to change our life. What can you be thankful for in order to change any negative focus and increase your joy?

_____

_____

_____

_____

_____

_____

_____

_____

_____

3. Nehemiah 8:10 (NLT) says, "And Nehemiah continued, 'Go and celebrate with a feast of rich foods and sweet drinks, and share gifts of food with people who have nothing prepared. This is a sacred day before our Lord. Don't be dejected and sad, for the joy of the LORD is your strength!'" How does this scripture verse speak to you concerning your marriage?

_____

_____

_____

_____

_____

_____

_____

_____

_____

_____

_____

_____

_____

_____

_____

_____

_____

4. How big is God to you? John 14:6 (NLT) says, "Jesus told him, 'I am the way, the truth, and the life. No one can come to the Father except through me.'" Do you believe Jesus can heal and bring life to any aspect of your marriage?

_____

_____

_____

_____

_____

_____

_____

_____

_____

_____

_____

_____

_____

_____

_____

_____

_____

_____

_____

_____

God is Powerful

2

Change the Heart and the Body Will Follow

John 14:6 *(NLT)*
Jesus told him, "I am the way, the truth, and the life. No one can come to the Father except through me.

A very important aspect of allowing God and His Kingdom to transform your life and marriage is to recognize that there are facts in life, and then there are God's truths. Sometimes they are the same, but often, they are not; especially in the beginning of the restoration process. Let me give you a few examples:

FACT: My spouse has left.

TRUTH: God goes after the lost and brings them home.

Luke 15: 4 *(NIV)*
Suppose one of you has a hundred sheep and loses one of them. Doesn't he leave the ninety-nine in the open country and go after the lost sheep until he finds it?

11

FACT: I am getting a divorce.

TRUTH: The marriage covenant is more than just a piece of paper. God was present at your marriage. You and your spouse are in covenant with the Lord when you get married. Because God created marriage; therefore, your marriage is His.

Ezekiel 16:8 (NLT)

And when I passed by again, I saw that you were old enough for love. So I wrapped my cloak around you to cover your nakedness and declared my marriage vows. I made a covenant with you, says the Sovereign LORD, and you became mine.

FACT: My spouse said they don't love me anymore.

TRUTH: God's love for you is the ultimate love. When you allow His love to fill you first, the hurt of your spouse saying they don't love you does not keep you from feeling loved.

1 John 4:16 (NIV)

And so we know and rely on the love God has for us. God is love. Whoever lives in love lives in God, and God in them.

It is common to hear people's opinion regarding your marriage especially excuses of why you need to move on, "Well, you can't make someone love you; everyone has free will." It is a moot point. The **truth** is: God can change the heart of any spouse and where the heart goes, the body will follow.

Proverbs 21:1 (NLT)

The king's heart is like a stream of water directed by the LORD; He guides it wherever He pleases.

I want to reiterate that we cannot change a person's will. If God won't, we cannot assume we can. God is after people's hearts, and we can pray that God will change your spouse's heart, because that is truly what we want to see. A changed and transformed heart is what brings spouses home, whether physically or emotionally.

After years of not loving my husband, Neil, as God would have me love him, he had become quite hard-hearted. I was quite the nagging wife; always thinking I knew how to do things better and quick to point out things he was doing incorrectly. While we were separated, God really challenged me on loving my husband well, whether deserved or undeserved. I will elaborate more in another chapter, but I had to rely on God that he would open up doors of opportunity for me to show my husband love. This was challenging as we had no shared activities, no kids, nothing to connect us. I continued to pray that Jesus would help me recognize the open doors, in order to be faithful to sow seeds of love and trust that God would turn them into a stream of love.

Showing Neil love came in many forms, but the two areas I worked on were food – making his lunch and dinner – and ironing his clothes, because at the time, the uniform for the job he had looked best ironed. So when God gave me the opportunity to invite him over for dinner and he accepted, I made sure to make something he really liked, and I told him beforehand to bring over his uniforms, as I would be happy to iron them for him. To this day, Neil still tells this story when people ask him why he came home. His heart started to turn because it was feeling loved. God gave me the heart to do the things I needed to do in order to bring about this redirection.

I challenge you to ask God for areas in your heart that need to turn so that you can love your spouse with your whole heart. Everything is about choice. You may prefer to do things a certain way, but that certain way may bring up a wall between you and your spouse. For example, I like to have the dishes loaded a certain way in the dish washer. Neil has his own way of loading the dishwasher. If Neil blesses me by doing the dishes but it's not the way I would do it, I can choose to be upset, redo the way it's done, and complain that he didn't do it correctly. Or I can receive the blessing and love Neil is giving. I can choose to know it is not going to kill the dishes if they face the wrong way or that it isn't optimized in the dishwasher. (Ladies you know what I'm saying here, let it go!) What is more important... that you have your way, or that your relationship with your spouse flows in love? If you are struggling in an area that you know you should let go of, ask the Holy Spirit for help. God doesn't leave us on our own to change what is needed in order to be restored to a healthy marriage. He is your best ally! Plus, His help comes with the power to tear down walls and build up strong towers of His truth in your heart, life and marriage. So begin asking, and watch as what Jesus paid for at the cross starts flowing into your relationship!

Be Encouraged

(Testimony by Carlia)

Sharon and Neil's testimony will forever be a part of my own love story. I'll never forget the day I heard it. I had 'known' Neil and Sharon for years— seen their family grow, their marriage flourish, and known their hearts to serve and to love Jesus. Still, I had never heard the story of their separation, and it came as a bit of a shock to me. Having only witnessed the restored, post-Jesus side of their lives, it was, honestly, hard to imagine the broken people in their story could have actually been them. Beyond my obvious praise and excitement for them, a scary truth began to set in: Sharon's testimony reminded me more of myself, and the potential path of my own marriage.

I had only been married two years at the time, but the strains of my lacking as a wife were already clear. Like Neil, my husband grew up with a mother who ran a very tidy household, home-cooked meals, never a dirty dish or laundry pile unattended to, and everything in its proper place. An incredible mother, no doubt, but far from my own natural desire or ability. There was never a disagreement in our house that didn't stem from the list of chores I'd abandoned or the pile of clothes I had allowed to sit all week. But Sharon's story brought me hope. With God working through her, she was able to adopt a servant's heart toward her husband, and became the wife he so deeply desired. Because He had done this in their marriage, I knew He would do it again in mine.

I began to pray for a change in me, for the dread I felt in cleaning to become joy. That my love for my husband would eclipse any spirit of laziness or apathy. And sure enough, God met me where I was, and began to lead me toward the wife I longed to be. Instead of repeatedly waiting for the arguments to begin when the mess became too unbearable, I finally learned the art of cleaning as I went, and shocked my husband in the process. I quickly learned that the duties I had despised (and so eagerly avoided) were seen as acts of love in my husband's eyes. While I'll admit it's still an ongoing battle in my flesh, God has brought me infinitely closer to the wife my husband needs, and I'm so grateful He did it through Sharon's testimony. I'll forever be changed and inspired by the journey the Migala's endured, and the love they continue to hold.

Walk In It

Sit down and think about two areas in your life that you and your spouse disagree upon. Ask God for ways that love can be introduced into the situation, and what you can do to bring that into being. If your heart needs to change first before you're willing to do anything about it, lead your conversation with asking God for help. Ask Him to show you that you can trust Him in this area, and you are loved so much that it's okay to let your way go.

Power

Ezekiel 36:26 (*NLT*)
And I will give you a new heart, and I will put a new spirit in you. I will take out your stony, stubborn heart and give you a tender, responsive heart.

Psalm 119:160 (*NLT*)
The very essence of your words is truth; all your just regulations will stand forever.

Some Things to Think About

1. Write down 3 FACTS about your marriage that need to change to line up with God's Word. Then, do an online search to find 3 scriptures that give God's TRUTH on those subjects. Write down the TRUTH and make a new habit of declaring those truths daily over yourself and your marriage.

_____

_____

_____

_____

_____

_____

_____

_____

_____

_____

_____

_____

_____

_____

_____

_____

_____

_____

_____

2. Ask the Holy Spirit for one area of your heart that needs a change in order for your marriage to be strengthened. Write it down.

_____

_____

_____

_____

_____

_____

_____

_____

_____

_____

_____

_____

_____

_____

_____

_____

_____

_____

_____

_____

_____

_____

3. Jesus is the way, the truth and the life. When you are ready to bring life to the area of your heart that needs a change, ask Him for ideas on ways to go about bringing this change. Be patient with yourself and your spouse. Restoration is a process and God is bigger than our first steps that may be unbalanced and awkward. Trust Him that as you step out He will get you where you need to be. Write down ideas and then come back later to make notes as to how they went. Continue to ask Jesus for new ideas. May journaling on the lines below be the start of ideas that lead you to your testimony of a healed marriage.

_____

_____

_____

_____

_____

_____

_____

_____

_____

_____

_____

_____

_____

_____

_____

_____

Your Heart

Proverbs 4:23(NLT)
Watch over your heart with all diligence,
For from it flow the springs of life.

Have you ever had a fight with your spouse and suddenly you feel emotionally cut off from them, wondering how you ever felt a connection to them in the first place? When we have had fight after fight with our spouse and our focus has been all about how we feel and how we are hurt, love cannot flow from us. We build emotional walls, and stockpile hurtful words so the next time we are in those situations, we can protect ourselves. This is what it looks like to no longer have life (the power and love of God) flowing from your heart; your heart is missing the continual healing that the life of Jesus provides, and bitterness and hurt can easily penetrate it.

Most likely, if you are reading this book, you need some healing in order to understand the truths about your heart, its purpose and what the Word of God has to say about it. The desire to love and be loved is something we all can understand; however, depending on where life finds you, you may not have any feeling of love whatsoever. The word numb comes to mind as to how you may be feeling. But we were made for love, to love, and for relationships; most important of all, our relationship with our Father in Heaven. It is out of this relationship that our purpose to love flows in and out. This is why it is so very important to guard your heart.

I've seen many different ways to go about the healing of your heart, and honestly, there has been merit to many of them. My journey of heart healing has been exactly that...a journey. Many different approaches (roads) have been taken that have lead me to this point of sharing the things I have learned so as to encourage you. May what I have learned help you in your journey to stay in the flow of love, even when things come and try to block your path.

Thirteen years ago, from the printing of this book, when this journey of restoration began, my friend (the one that kicked me in the butt with the Lazarus story) was also searching for answers to help other couples find marriage restoration. She suggested I try a counseling session with someone where I look through my past, confess any wrongs I had done, ask for forgiveness and put it under the blood of Jesus. I found it beneficial to confess my sins, but it was missing the intimacy of having God speak to me specifically what I need to let go of and confess through a process of meeting with Him daily. Him knowing when and how freedom from anything I was holding onto needed to take place.

God is the ultimate healer, counselor and friend. Plus, He has been there at every moment of your life and He can bring up any situation that needs to be dealt with because He doesn't bury memories like we do. He redeems them.

We each NEED quiet time with God. What that looks like is different for everyone. You may find you are the type of person that likes to connect with God one specific way, or you may be like me and find your life needs each day tailored to itself. There is no right or wrong way. What is important is the connection to God and hearing what He has to say to you.

My life is quite full. I have my family to care for and each of them need my time and love. I serve in all sorts of ways through our church, and my weekdays are filled with homeschooling and regular responsibilities that come with running a household. I could say I am too busy for all this quiet time and healing, but that would not be wise. It is all about priorities, and seeing what needs to be first in order for me to walk in strength and love in the other areas of my life. If I do not place time with the One that created me as a priority, then the things that I need to or want to do will be done with less strength. A healed, unblocked heart is the well-spring of your life, so making your heart and its healing a priority is worth the investment.

I mentioned earlier that my time with God is tailored daily. Often, I can start my day reading a chapter of the Bible and making a few observations about it. Last year, I started following a program through our church's women's ministry called S.O.A.P. (an acronym for Scripture, Observation, Application and Prayer). This is a method of reading the Bible and journaling your observations about the chapter you are reading. I have found this to be an easy way to connect to the Holy Spirit, and begin my day in strength.

(If you would like more information on S.O.A.P., there are many online resources. One link I found useful is http://soapstudy.com)

During school and chore time, I will play praise and worship music. Sometimes it is to keep calm in our home, and other times it is to bring the Lord's energy and joy. Our whole family will dance together and sing aloud. Praise music is an atmosphere changer.

Another day, you may find me laying on my bed, just staring to heaven in absolute quiet. It gives me a pause in what could be a tough day, and reminds me that God is with me and I'm not alone.

I can be standing at the kitchen sink and something rises up in me and says, just say hi to Jesus. You need to remember you don't just go through life to get through it. Jesus is there to be your friend and bring a smile to your face and mind. Every time I pause and say hi to Jesus, I can't help but smile. It's like a private moment between friends.

At the end of the day, it can be easy for me to crash and lose out on another connection point with God. I have been using bedtime prayers with my children to help them establish a routine of hearing from Jesus and for me to remember to not rush through bedtime prayers. My boys each take a moment and ask Jesus what He would like to talk about.

I have also used bedtime as a time for the boys to soak with some soft worship music and finish their day focusing on the presence of God filling their room. (See Chapter 6 for more on soaking)

Whatever the day brings, I don't condemn myself for not doing this or that. It is a joy to connect with Jesus and the more opportunities I give myself to do that, the more likely I will keep it as a priority. Life flows through me the more I connect with God.

Trusting God So You Can Enjoy Your Life Right Now

Psalm 37:1-6 (NLT)
Don't worry about the wicked
or envy those who do wrong.
² For like grass, they soon fade away.
Like spring flowers, they soon wither.
³ Trust in the LORD and do good.
Then you will live safely in the land and prosper.
⁴ Take delight in the LORD,
and He will give you your heart's desires.
⁵ Commit everything you do to the LORD.
Trust Him, and He will help you.
⁶ He will make your innocence radiate like the dawn,
and the justice of your cause will shine like the noonday sun.

James 1:2 says, "Consider it pure joy, my brothers and sisters, whenever you face trials of many kinds," (NIV). This scripture is one that usually makes me shake my head and think, "Well, that's a really good thought, but I wonder if I'll ever get there." One day, I was reading the New Living Translation of that same verse, and a deeper revelation of its true meaning sprung up in me. The New Living

Translation says, "Dear brothers and sisters, when troubles
come your way, consider it an *opportunity* for great joy,"
(italics are mine for emphasis). I think this is exactly what
James was saying in that scripture verse about *counting* it
all joy. It is not that the circumstances around you are
always joyful and that you should count them as such. If
that was the case, Jesus wouldn't have shown us to pray
for Earth to reflect Heaven. But we weren't meant to get
through by the skin of our teeth or to endure life in order to
note all the good that came out of terrible situations and
find joy and comfort in that. Rather, it is that there is an
opportunity to find joy in all seasons of life.

My life may not be exactly how I envisioned it to be. I have
a vision of all sorts of good things God wants me to have in
this life but I may not be fully experiencing it yet. God has
actually provided a way to have fun and experience joy in
hard moments or trials. The basis for all true things starts
with the Bible. In Psalm 37 it says, "Commit everything you
do to the LORD. Trust him, and He will help you." When
things aren't as you envision they should be, remember to
commit it all to the Lord, trust Him to move you out of areas
that aren't looking like Heaven, and know that He will help
you.

Jesus didn't die on the cross for just my future days. He
died on the cross for me to have good days right now. And
if I'm keeping my eye on God's plan of why I am at any
particular place, I can see how God wants me to enjoy
being in His purpose. (More on this in Chapter 4)

Instead of focusing on all the negatives of having children,
I can choose to enjoy my kids. I can remember that I have
a purpose in teaching them and doing life with them every

day. There are days when I want to stress over maintaining a schedule and trying to get everything done that I had planned. My other choice is that I can enjoy the moments when they're being silly, or they're telling me some random story they are so excited to share. It's about taking a pause in those moments and smiling and laughing. Understand, that you have the power to decide what you make important, and it's that decision that can determine whether the moment is positive or negative, no matter what the moment is. We all need to find more opportunities to smile or laugh. There is life (the power and love of God) in it.

So how do you find opportunities to grow in this? I'm glad you asked. You can find, what I like to call, God-purpose in your life just by smiling more, or even looking for ways to love on people by paying someone a nice compliment. There is fun to be had in doing good things, and you can trust God in those moments, whether the person you complimented received the kind thing you did or not.

Joy comes from doing what God wants you to do and being happy that you're doing it. There is a freedom there. I don't have to worry if a friend is going to like me or if my spouse is going to reciprocate the love I am putting out there, because God is taking care of my heart. I can see that it is so much better to be humble and love others first instead of myself. God sees you and says well done, now enjoy that you are doing good stuff!

It can be easy to get swallowed up by all that is going on in our world today, but if you can understand that God will take care of your heart, it will help keep His love flowing to you, and out of you to others.

Be Encouraged

(Testimony by Karen)

Finding out my husband was cheating on me made me feel deeply hurt, alone and angry! We went into counseling immediately, where our pastor mentioned, "Karen, if you want to divorce Don, according to God's Word, here's your reason. You are free to do so. Here's your way out." Through the tremendous pain I was feeling, I also felt something in me that didn't want to divorce him. Our pastor led us to Sharon, who spoke God's words to me, nothing more, nothing less. She spoke perfect Biblical truths to me, and showed me in the Word that love was a better way of living, instead of judgment. I just listened and cried. Cried from the pain and cried that a stranger cared enough to not give me her opinion on the matter, or what the world would tell me, but rather what God would tell me.

In my pain though, I wanted Don to feel pain too. I was tempted to tell my friends and family and expose him. I wanted them to know the facts about him and for them to agree with how horrible he was, and how I deserved better. But amidst of the temptation to expose him, I heard a small, inaudible voice inside of me that said, "You only want to tell them because you are suffering now, and you want people to pity you. Even if you do tell them, they will only tell you how to deal with your situation based on how they would react if this had happened to them. They live by their feelings, and not by God's will. There is no way they can help you, Karen." I believe that was God imparting His divine wisdom to me. He knew I didn't need a pity party and He knew exposing Don would not help my pain go away. My heart needed to be healed, so that love could flow through it.

I decided not to expose his sin, not only because I knew I would regret it later, but also because the Bible says that "love covers" one another. The last thing I wanted to do was cover my husband who hurt me so badly, but God knows better than I do and I chose to listen to Him, and His powerful Word, and not my feelings.

At the time of the writing of this book, it has been three years and I'm glad to say that I have still "covered" him in love. I feel a sense of responsibility to protect him and that's because God used my husband's sin to change my heart and no person on earth could've done that for me. That is what makes God so great. He uses the hard stuff to soften us.

Today I can thank God for making me stronger through this trial, for softening my heart, for increasing my compassion for my husband and increasing my faith in Him. I believe that when we let God lead our marriage, we can expect miracles within our marriage.

Walk In It

Look at your calendar, and schedule one-on-one time with God. Length of time, where, and how is up to you. Do what you are comfortable with. This is not a tool to bring about condemnation or one more thing to do, but a tool to bring about a regular way of replenishing yourself. God loves you, knows you and wants to set you free from anything that is holding you back from a life of freedom.

Power

Proverbs 4:23-27 (MSG)

[23-27] *Keep vigilant watch over your heart;*

that's where life starts.

Don't talk out of both sides of your mouth;

avoid careless banter, white lies, and gossip.

Keep your eyes straight ahead;

ignore all sideshow distractions.

Watch your step,

and the road will stretch out smooth before you.

Look neither right nor left;

leave evil in the dust.

Some Things to Think About

1. Does love flow through your heart? Oftentimes, we have things that will trigger an emotional "wall" or "dam" to stop love from flowing into and through us. Being aware of what these triggers are is a powerful step toward keeping them from going up. The next time you find yourself in a situation where you don't want to be nice, ask yourself, "What am I feeling right now?" Shame, rejection, anger? Write down these feelings so you can talk to the Holy Spirit about what is true about the actual situation, what is really triggering the emotion(s), and how to release them. We weren't meant to carry negative emotions. Invite Holy Spirit in to comfort and heal.

_____

_____

_____

_____

_____

_____

_____

_____

_____

_____

_____

_____

2. During or after your first soaking time with Jesus, journal some observations about the experience. Was this all new to you? Did you hear something special? Was this a new way for you to experience God on a regular basis?

_____

_____

_____

_____

_____

_____

_____

_____

_____

_____

_____

_____

_____

_____

_____

_____

_____

_____

3. Write down something about your spouse that you can appreciate or enjoy.

_____

_____

_____

_____

_____

_____

_____

_____

_____

_____

_____

_____

_____

_____

_____

_____

_____

_____

_____

_____

_____

_____

_____

_____

4. What can you do to show love to your spouse without expecting anything back in return? If your spouse feels love by touch, you could offer to give them a back or foot massage. If acts of service is appreciated, make a point to take care of something they usually do, like the trash or dishes, and do it for them. Challenge yourself to find a new way every week to show love without any strings attached.

_____

_____

_____

_____

_____

_____

_____

_____

_____

_____

_____

_____

_____

_____

_____

_____

_____

_____

_____

_____

_____

_____

_____

_____

_____

_____

_____

_____

_____

_____

_____

_____

_____

_____

_____

_____

_____

_____

_____

_____

_____

_____

4

Kingdom Viewpoint

John 18:36 (NLT)
Jesus answered, "My Kingdom is not an earthly kingdom. If it were, my followers would fight to keep me from being handed over to the Jewish leaders. But my Kingdom is not of this world."

Have you ever wondered why you're here? Do you think you are more of an accident or just an afterthought? It could be that you think you have purpose but you don't really know what it is. The Bible says that we were each created and placed here in time for this particular time and purpose.

Esther 4:14 (NIV)
14 For if you remain silent at this time, relief and deliverance for the Jews will arise from another place, but you and your father's family will perish. And who knows but that you have come to your royal position for such a time as this?"

Ephesians 1:11 (NIV)
In him we were also chosen, having been predestined according
to the plan of Him who works out everything in conformity with
the purpose of His will.

God didn't just place you here randomly or think maybe you will do pretty well here so let's send him or her down to earth now. It's not a case of maybe your number just came up and it was time for you to be born. You were born because of the particular gifts that God has put in you. He knew you before you were even born.

Psalm 139:13-16 (MSG)
Oh yes, you shaped me first inside, then out;
you formed me in my mother's womb.
I thank you, High God—you're breathtaking!
Body and soul, I am marvelously made!
I worship in adoration—what a creation!
You know me inside and out,
you know every bone in my body;
You know exactly how I was made, bit by bit,
how I was sculpted from nothing into something.
Like an open book, you watched me grow from conception to
birth;
all the stages of my life were spread out before you,
The days of my life all prepared
before I'd even lived one day.

You may think, "I would've been better off born in 1940 or in the 18th century." But God's truth is that you were born with particular skills and He has a purpose for them in this exact moment in time. Unfortunately, very few people have had that realization.

Maybe you feel you do have a purpose, but you don't know what it is. One way to start exploring your purpose and to find ways to dive into those areas is to sit down and ask yourself "How do I view God?" There are many ways to see God; examples being a father figure, deliverer, friend or healer (although there are many more ways).

Depending on your life experiences, you may or may not have a distorted view of God. Task master or distant may come to mind. Whether your viewpoint is positive or negative, you can take this information and step into a wonderful new relationship with God. Couple your first question with a second one like, "How would I like to see God?" The answer you get can help you find scripture verses focusing on how you'd like to see God. For example, if your answer were healer, you would then look up all the times Jesus healed. Just by getting familiar with what the Word of God says regarding that answer, you can rest, knowing you just discovered another aspect of who God is to you.

John 14:9 (NIV)
Jesus answered: "Don't you know me, Philip, even after I have been among you such a long time? Anyone who has seen me has seen the Father. How can you say, 'Show us the Father'?

It is a journey discovering the many facets of God and truly how awesome He is. As you allow God to renew your mind and change your perspective of Him, you will start to understand what your own gifts are. Now you may be asking, how does discovering who God is help me understand my gifts? To better explain this concept, if you see God as a healer, or you'd like to see God as a healer, than it is very likely that you have a gifting and heart to see others healed. You can start stepping out and praying for people to receive what Jesus has paid for us to have. Using this viewpoint of God as a healer can fulfill you as you step out and bring those aspects of God to other people.

Personally, I see God as a redeemer, a restorer, a healer, a deliverer and my friend. I have a love for seeing marriages and relationships restored and redeemed. I love praying for people to be healed. I have a heart to be a really good friend. I find joy in sharing how good a friend God is, how big He is, and that He restores, redeems and heals. Because I see God in this way, these are the areas that I focus on when sharing my truth to others. As you learn to see and know who God is to you, you will in turn have a platform to be able to share those truths with those you come in contact.

Purpose in the Kingdom

Revelation 21:3-4 *(ESV)*
"Behold, the dwelling place of God is with man. He will dwell with them, and they will be his people, and God himself will be with them as their God. He will wipe away every tear from their eyes, and death shall be no more, neither shall there be mourning, nor crying, nor pain anymore, for the former things have passed away."

Knowing your purpose helps you to see every situation that you are in as an opportunity for the Kingdom of God to be here on earth. For example, you may be going to a party but may not really want to go, or maybe you don't know anyone, or there are people there you don't feel particularly close to. Instead of trying to "survive" the party, you can ask yourself, "Do I have purpose in going? Can I use the good things God has in me to bless someone else?" Allow the Holy Spirit to speak to you, and then go out with a Kingdom purpose and see what God will do.

Going to the party with Kingdom purpose could play out like this. You could seek out another person who does not know anyone and bless them with a good conversation. Or maybe you could pray for someone. You could even show up to the party and let the host know you that you appreciated them opening their home.

Being purposeful doesn't have to be a huge event...it could be something very small, but done with intention. I know I can change my attitude about going somewhere or being somewhere if I ask myself this simple question, "What is God's purpose for me to be there?" I am intentional in looking for opportunities to bless somebody, to take my focus off myself and start looking at who else is here and needs to be blessed. How can I bring Heaven to Earth here in this moment for them to experience God? And it's truly amazing that I can go home feeling great by getting my focus off of me and onto someone else! That is what purpose is all about.

Purpose in Your Marriage

Now that you see you can have purpose in everyday situations, let me apply this to marriage.

How you view your spouse, your situation and life, determines how much love you will walk in. Does how you feel rule the things you say and do? When you feel bad, do you say negative things, and agree with the feelings that are going on inside of you? When your spouse does things that hurt you, and you spew harsh words, this will add another brick to the emotional wall that is coming between the both of you. Perhaps, you tend to disengage completely, and intentionally withdraw yourself and your love from your spouse. It can be a nasty negative cycle.

There is another viewpoint, and with it, comes an end to the vicious negative cycles and huge walls that cut you off from love and healing. It is God's viewpoint, or what I like to refer to as Kingdom viewpoint. Kingdom viewpoint is viewing everything you do and who you come in contact with through the lens of God's Kingdom. This viewpoint allows you to see God's plans for you and your marriage or situation and how you can walk in love in the midst of it.

Matthew 6:33 (NIV)
But seek first His kingdom and His righteousness, and all these things will be given to you as well.

In order to walk in love, we have to stop and ask what would Jesus like to do in this situation. By seeking first His Kingdom, which is simply going to God in prayer and asking how can I help usher His love into that moment so that healing can flow, all that you will need for the situation will be added to you. Even though it is natural for us to want to protect our feelings or retaliate, it is when we stop and choose God's way of dealing with things that we get to see supernatural results in our life.

Ephesians 5:21-28 (MSG)

Out of respect for Christ, be courteously reverent to one another. Wives, understand and support your husbands in ways that show your support for Christ. The husband provides leadership to his wife the way Christ does to his church, not by domineering but by cherishing. So just as the church submits to Christ as He exercises such leadership, wives should likewise submit to their husbands.

Husbands, go all out in your love for your wives, exactly as Christ did for the church—a love marked by giving, not getting. Christ's love makes the church whole. His words evoke her beauty. Everything He does and says is designed to bring the best out of her, dressing her in dazzling white silk, radiant with holiness. And that is how husbands ought to love their wives. They're really doing themselves a favor—since they're already "one" in marriage.

Wives, what is it that you really want out of your marriage? I know I want to feel loved and know my husband, whom I chose to be with, wants to be with me. My heart longs for him to value what I value. Most women want the same thing.

Husbands, what is it that you really want out of your marriage? I know when I get self-absorbed in the things that need to be done or that I want done, respect for what my husband finds important is his number one complaint. In acknowledging the importance of our own wants, we should then acknowledge our responsibility to value what our spouse values.

God, being our Creator, knows how we are wired, knows how we think, and knows how we will work best. As with everything God calls us to do, He provides a model in

Jesus. As Christ loved and submitted His own life to the church, so we should live by that example to love and submit to our spouse.

By first submitting to Christ, we learn how to submit to our spouse. Although our spouse is not perfect, we can trust that as we submit to Christ, who is perfect, that He will take the burden of trying to please our spouse and replace it with His blessings. The word submit often gets a bad rap because we only see it as yielding to another person's will. But if we look at the word submission it has two parts. Sub, meaning a smaller part of, and mission, a task or job someone is given to do. When you look at submit through the word submission you can see God's purpose for a marriage. To come under the same mission and work as a team with your spouse. Think about all the benefits of honoring Christ and His mission here on earth and the mission He has given you and your spouse. God created your spouse and for this very reason and they are valuable. Value the mission you have together in marriage.

Husbands, when you love your wife, you are not drawing from your own well of love, but an endless supply from God. You can choose to love your wife even if she is being unlovely or disrespectful. The outcome of your relationship is determined by your choices, how you think, and how you act. You can choose to think the best of your wife for the same reasons God thinks the best of you. He chose before the beginning of time to love us all. Lovely and unlovely, He knows the only way you will come to Him is because of His love. I pray this thought makes it easier to love.

A good friend of mine likes to say, "Just because something is hard doesn't make it bad; it's just hard!" Push through and make the hard choices. Love in all situations! When it comes to relationships, there are huge benefits to showing love, respect and valuing what your spouse does and giving everything you can to your relationship. God really does know best. So remember to keep your mind on His Kingdom Viewpoint.

Be Encouraged

(Testimony by Crystal)

"All of my life, in every season You are still God, I have a reason to sing, I have a reason to worship." These powerful words from the Desert song by Hillsong are just one of the many phrases God gave me to stand on during one of the toughest seasons in my life. Shortly after getting married, my husband, Kevin, and I saw how difficult marriage really was and thus began our roller coaster ride of a year.

We had gotten married a few years after high school (where we met and became high school sweethearts). We had many ups and downs, but pushed many issues aside and tied the knot believing things would change in time.

Only a few short months after getting married, Kevin began to pull away and then joined the military. We decided to see how the "separation" worked and go from there. At first, he wanted to work things out (once he was done with boot camp) and then shortly after being away at tech school, he said it was over. I couldn't believe it! Part of me was sad and hurt but wanted to fight for my marriage. The other part of me was mad over the many ups and downs we'd already had since the beginning of our relationship. It had been back and forth since we got married, and at this point I was over it and ready to move on.

A friend of mine had gone through a very similar situation and ended up getting divorced. She encouraged me to fight for my marriage and stand strong as she wished she had. I started praying again for Kevin (especially prayers from "The Power of a Praying Wife" by Stormie Omartian) and to seek God about our marriage. For months, I carried our marriage and my husband around like a burden and tried everything to change the situation in my own power, but I finally told the Lord, "I can't do this anymore, but You can! So take this marriage and transform us into the husband and wife you created us to be."

Once I really let go of it and gave it to the Lord, I immediately saw things start to change. Kevin agreed to go speak to a pastor friend who really encouraged us and we were able to start fresh from that point on. I know that if I hadn't given it to God, we would not be where we are today!

Walk In It

Close your eyes and envision Jesus before you. Tell Him you want your marriage to be fully in the Kingdom of God and for Him to transform you and your spouse so as to reflect it.

Power

John 15:16 (MSG)
You didn't choose me, remember; I chose you, and put you in the world to bear fruit, fruit that won't spoil. As fruit bearers, whatever you ask the Father in relation to me, He gives you.

Romans 14:17 (NIV)
For the kingdom of God is not a matter of eating and drinking, but of righteousness, peace and joy in the Holy Spirit,

Some Things to Think About

1. What does your mind primarily focus on…the things of the Kingdom of God or the things of this world? If your answer is the world, what is one area of your life that you would like to see through the lens of the Kingdom of God? Take time to think about what in you could change in order to have this one area reflect the Kingdom of God.

_____

_____

_____

_____

_____

_____

_____

_____

_____

_____

_____

_____

_____

_____

_____

_____

2. Write down how you would like to view God. Does this character trait sound like something you could find your purpose in? We all have many gifts and depending on your season of life, your purpose can change. Don't get hung up on future or past purposes. What can you do right now to walk in your purpose? Your purpose will bless both you and those that you would interact with. As you start to find purpose, continue to look for other areas of your life that could become a Kingdom purpose.

_____

_____

_____

_____

_____

_____

_____

_____

_____

_____

_____

_____

_____

_____

_____

_____

_____

_____

3. What is your purpose in your marriage? Showing love to your spouse is always one purpose of marriage. What are 3 ways you can strengthen your purpose for being married? Once you answer this question, make a separate copy of those 3 ways and put them somewhere you can see them as you get ready in the morning. Declare those things first thing every morning to yourself. Remind yourself that you have purpose in your marriage.

_____

_____

_____

_____

_____

_____

_____

_____

_____

_____

_____

_____

_____

_____

_____

_____

_____

_____

5

Jesus Paid it All

1 Corinthians 6:20 (NIV)
You were bought at a price. Therefore honor God with your bodies.

When you look at your marriage, do you tend to take all the responsibility for where it is at today? Do you feel guilty? Do you blame your spouse for the state of your marriage? When Neil and I were separated, I felt horrible for my part of the failures. I had not been a loving wife. I often tried to 'fix' my husband so he would act the way I felt he should. I did not value his love languages nor did I make it a priority to show love in those ways.

As I journeyed on my path toward a resurrected marriage, I realized I first had to forgive myself for my part in our problems. And as I continued to spend time with Jesus, He showed me that when I placed the guilt I was feeling higher than the price He paid at the cross, I was devaluing His gift. I did not need to hold onto the burden of guilt any longer. By holding onto the guilt, I realized I wasn't glorifying God. I was actually acknowledging the enemy of my heart, satan, and glorifying him.

1 John 4:10 (NLT)
This is real love—not that we loved God, but that He loved us and sent His Son as a sacrifice to take away our sins.

Once Jesus paid for human sin, the need for us to carry that burden or pay for it ourselves was finished. The only part we need to do in order to actually walk in this forgiveness is to leave whatever sin you committed at the foot of the cross, repent, give it to Jesus and let it go. Then you can walk free of it.

So what about your spouse? Do you see their sin, their shortcomings, and failures as something bigger than what Jesus paid for on the cross? Is it a struggle for you? Have you ever considered forgiving your spouse?

Their sins are no bigger than yours or anyone else's. Jesus paid for all sin. We would all fall short of being in the glory of God, no matter what our sin. There are no levels to sin. We all need Jesus and the sooner we stop placing sin on levels of acceptability, the sooner we can see that our marriage can be healed.

Forgiveness is so important that Jesus actually tells us we must forgive in order to receive God's forgiveness.

Matthew 6:15 (NLT)
But if you refuse to forgive others, your Father will not forgive your sins.

How can this be? It sounds contrary to the God of love and forgiveness, but it's not. When we don't forgive, we are judging that person as well as ourselves. If the standard you give is unforgiveness, than that is the standard that you will be given. Take a step back and see the true picture. If the law is where you want to live, you are choosing to be judged for whatever good or bad that you do. No one is blemish free except the lamb of God, Jesus. Which do you want? To be forgiven for every sin you have ever done or to be judged? You cannot live in the knowledge of good and evil and expect the tree of life to be your reward.

God knows that when we don't forgive, bitterness sets in and thus gives way to a root that separates us from the good God has for us.

Forgiveness is not something you just give for a first offense; Jesus tells us to keep on forgiving.

Matthew 18:21-22 (NLT)
Then Peter came to him and asked, "Lord, how often should I forgive someone[1] who sins against me? Seven times?"
22 "No, not seven times," Jesus replied, "but seventy times seven!"

Don't be legalistic with this scripture. Jesus always teaches us to go to the higher level. Seventy times seven is not the end quota for forgiveness, but an illustration that we don't stop forgiving at any number that we think is reasonable like 7.

When we are wronged, we must choose to forgive. The longer we wait to forgive, the unforgiveness we are holding onto starts to take root in our hearts, which ends up leaving us bitter towards the person and the situation. Forgiving doesn't mean you have to trust that person again. It doesn't mean you will be immediately free from the hurt and the emotion that comes with it. The next step after giving forgiveness is letting Jesus heal your heart.

Forgiveness simply means you choose to wipe the slate clean and not to bring it up again. The one you have forgiven no longer has to pay for the wrong. You can't say you forgive them and then continue to bring it back up. Forgiveness is as if it never happened. God judges us as righteous when we are forgiven. God expects us to do the same.

One thing my husband, Neil, mentions when he gives our testimony is that I never would bring up things he did wrong. It was something that allowed his heart back into the marriage. The first time I heard him say this, I was greatly impacted as to the importance of forgiveness.

I would love to say that, yes, I always gave forgiveness freely, and was able to hand to Jesus any situation where I felt wronged, but this wasn't always the case. The one thing I was usually able to do was keep my mouth shut. I made the decision to not throw mistakes back at my husband because I knew my life was far from perfect and God didn't do that to me. As I read more scriptures on forgiveness, I learned forgiveness was not a choice, but something I had to do.

It took time to learn how to have a healed heart and to learn the importance of removing bitterness which was a result of the unforgiveness I was holding onto. God meets you where you are. It is our willingness to be conformed to the Word of God that brings about the transformation in us and our marriages.

Be Encouraged

(Testimony by Tania)

I was not raised to know and serve the Lord but I did have a vague idea of Him. My grandmother was a Christian and she used to speak truth into my life by always telling me that there is power in the blood of Christ. This thought was something that I would repeat to myself when fear would come against me.

My parents fought a lot as I was growing up, so I escaped the anger and found a sense of "happiness" by hanging out with my friends. Though it was fun, I always felt an emptiness inside. Sometimes, I would pray as modeled by my Grandmother. Even though I didn't know God, when I prayed, a sense of peace came upon me.

Not knowing that I was loved and precious to my Father in Heaven, I looked for love elsewhere and found my husband, Roberto. When I turned 18, we married and we were excited to start a family. I started attending church and learning about God. I was praying I would have a daughter to love. For some reason I wasn't getting pregnant and a doctor told me I wasn't able to have children. Because I didn't know about how God heals and always wants the best for us, I became angry with Him instead of trusting Him.

By the grace of God's goodness, I became pregnant against my diagnosis. I was so very grateful. Once my daughter arrived, The Holy Spirit challenged me to teach her about Jesus. It was then that I realized that I can't teach something that I don't know myself. So I surrendered myself to Christ and accepted Jesus as my Lord and Savior. I had a newfound expectancy for God to do good things.

I thought my husband would feel the same way about Jesus as I did, but unfortunately we were not at the same place. During this time, we were not trying to have any more children and I ended up having some complications from a birth-control method I was using. I had dealt with depression as a child and between being in disagreement with my husband about using this birth control and my hormones going crazy, I could find no peace. I ended up admitting myself to a mental institution.

Unfortunately, this was just one of the issues that my husband and I were having in our marriage. We had no firm foundation in Jesus and it showed. We ended up separating and soon after, my husband served me divorce paper. The battle for custody of our daughter began.

I wanted to hate him as my heart hurt for my daughter with all the conflict. I was not given much hope from my lawyer because of my history with mental illness. I knew God was still with me and He was faithful, so I decided to let go and let God and believe that He would work this out for His greater good.

I prayed to God that He would help me let go of the hate, to heal my heart and hormones, and for me to forgive Roberto so that we could, at the very least, raise our daughter without her walking in the same hatred.

One day I was reading Matthew 18:23-35 and it jumped off the page to me. It said that forgiveness is not optional but something we have to do for ourselves and so I decided then and there that I would forgive my husband for all the hurt that I felt. I decided I would be his friend and that we would have a good relationship with our daughter. I received favor from the court after this and we were able to come to an agreement for a good schedule of sharing our daughter.

Any time that I was away from my daughter, I spent seeking more of Jesus. I prayed for Roberto, not because I wanted him back, but because I wanted his soul to be saved and for Christ to be in his heart. I wanted the father of my daughter to go to heaven and to realize his purpose in this world. I often invited him to church. At first, he always had an excuse, but slowly his heart began to change and he accepted my invitation. After church, we would go get something to eat and this turned into dating. My daughter would ask him to pray before we ate and as I saw Christ in Roberto, my heart began to turn towards my husband. We continued to share custody and go out on the weekends as a family, but since our divorce was final, we lived separately.

The wonderful day came when my husband gave his life to Christ. I fell in love with him then like never before. I believed that the covenant that we had made with God was still true and that before God, we were still married.

We had planned to slowly ease into our relationship, but it didn't work out that way. I ended up getting pregnant and felt badly that my husband wasn't ready to remarry. I did not give up, but kept on praying about it and waited as the Lord worked on his heart. The day came when Roberto proposed and we ended up having the wedding that we never had before. We had come full circle and both of us decided to invite Jesus into our marriage and have Him as the center of our lives and family. Things are not perfect, but we are stronger and are now walking with Jesus as a couple, parents and as partners in this life.

Walk In It

Do you have any unforgiveness in your heart? Ask the Holy Spirit to give you insight into any situation where you need to walk in forgiveness. Choose to forgive and let Jesus help you walk free of bitterness.

Power

Hebrews 10:23 *(NIV)*
Let us hold unswervingly to the hope we profess, for He who promised is faithful.

Some Things to Think About

1. Forgiveness can often be needed daily when a marriage is at odds. Write down one thing you need to forgive yourself for when it comes to the state of your marriage. Choose to give yourself the grace God has provided. Ask the Holy Spirit for ideas on how not to repeat that offense.

_____

_____

_____

_____

_____

_____

_____

_____

_____

_____

_____

_____

_____

_____

_____

_____

_____

_____

2. Depending on how you feel love, there will be certain things that your spouse does that may seem unforgiveable because it hurts down to your very core. Pray for the strength and love to forgive quickly when these things come up. God is awesome and not only does He provide freedom, but He provides restoration. Write down a prayer that you can pray daily for your spouse so they can do the opposite of the actions that cause you to hurt. For example, if harsh words really hurt you, pray that the Lord will fill their speech with love and kindness.

_____

_____

_____

_____

_____

_____

_____

_____

_____

_____

_____

_____

_____

_____

_____

_____

3. Search the internet for what the Bible says about the area you prayed about in the previous question. Sites like www.biblegateway.com have keyword searches available. For example, I looked up "*speaking*" and it brought up many scriptures on what the Bible says about speaking. Ephesians 4:29 (NIV) stood out to me, "Do not let any unwholesome talk come out of your mouths, but only what is helpful for building others up according to their needs, that it may benefit those who listen." Use your scripture verse to write a declaration about your spouse. Insert your spouse's name into anywhere that fits. In this scripture, I could insert a name in place of the word "any" and it would be a powerful declaration of life over whomever I was saying it for. Write yours out here.

_____

_____

_____

_____

_____

_____

_____

_____

_____

_____

_____

_____

_____

6

God is Your Husband

Isaiah 54:5 *(NASB)*
For your husband is your Maker, Whose name is the Lord of host, And your Redeemer is the Holy One of Israel, Who is called the God of all the earth.

Whether you are a man or woman, God can be what you need at any time. You may be married, separated, divorced or living in the same house, but not functioning as true intimate partners in life; God can be the deliverer of that intimacy.

We each feel love differently. Each part of our being (mind, body, emotions) can be loved in a special way. These are called our love languages. Have you heard of The 5 Love Languages? Dr. Gary Chapman and Dr. Ross Campbell, M.D., created a resource that helps you understand how you receive love best, as well as how you show love to others. You can get that resource by going to www.focusonthefamily.com and looking up "Understanding the Five Love Languages."

Having an understanding of your own love language and your spouse's will give a jumpstart on re-establishing the bonds of intimacy. In the meantime, as you navigate your journey, allow God to satisfy all of your love needs. God is love. He created love and He created us. I believe He is well-qualified.

How can God in heaven meet these needs? It may be that He fulfills your love language by inspiring some friends to send you flowers or a nice note. If spending quality time is of value to you God may prompt a friend to bring you lunch and stay to chat with you.

Jesus is always with us. He never leaves you and just being aware of His presence can fill you up when you feel your spouse is leaving you empty. Maybe you haven't noticed that you are not acknowledging that Jesus is with you. Now is a great time to choose to spend a few moments soaking in His presence. As I've mentioned before, soaking is just a term to describe entering into a restful time with the Lord. It can take on many forms. My favorite is to listen to some peaceful worship music and just imagine being with Jesus. You can also listen to scripture verses or have nothing playing at all. It is all about resting. It is not a time to strive or pray or ask for something. Just be with the one that created you and you will be amazed at how it heals and refreshes you. Length of time can vary. I would start with one song and then add on from there.

I challenge you if you are feeling empty in any area of your life, particularly if it is from a lack of connection with your spouse, connect with God. He wants to be your connection. He wants you to have a good connection with your spouse and it starts with connecting to true love, for God is love.

1 John 4:8(NIV)
*Whoever does not love does not know God, because **God is love.***

Maybe you're someone who loves surprises. You can ask God for surprises in His Word. You can read the Bible anytime and anywhere and find surprises! Words can just leap off the page to you when you come expecting to receive from the Holy Spirit. These are the things that will touch your heart and give you that fulfillment that you long to feel. You were created to connect with God and have Him be the source to feel loved.

When we decide to be married to somebody, we think that we will be fulfilled by their love for us. It is how the world around us portrays relationships. We see it in movies and we hear about it in songs. Worldly media wants to convince you that this is what will complete you.

Most of us acknowledge that this is not reality. If we've been married for any period of time, we also know that this type of infatuation just doesn't last. Love is a choice and you have to choose every day to love. It is just like the free will God gave us to have a relationship with Him and choose His ways. We can choose to love even when we're feeling unlovely or when we are an emotional wreck. It starts with acknowledging that emotions are not number one and we have control over our emotions, even if it sometimes feels like we're out of control. You can train yourself to reign in those unlovely emotions.

We know through God's word that God is patient and kind, so let's start there. If my husband is not being patient or kind, I may easily feel like I should not be patient or kind. The truth is we shouldn't be relying on another person to control how we react in any situation. When we are relying on God and His patience and kindness, whatever anybody is doing around us should not affect our emotional barometer. If I say I trust God and I know He is patient with me when I am unlovely, then I can love my spouse the same way when they are not at their most loveable moment.

Pause and reason that you can be patient and kind when things are not serene around you. With practice choosing not to retaliate, negative for negative, you can get to the point where you stay unruffled in crazy situations. You can automatically choose something loving to do, even if the most loving thing is to calmly walk away. It may be tough in the moment, but if you are looking for ways to defuse the bomb instead of allowing it to explode, walking away calmly will infuse love into a difficult situation. It may be clumsy at first; it's okay. Give yourself grace as God does. As you step out and stop looking for ways to even the score, you can then move into a period of purposefully loving. It is a great chance to love your spouse the way they feel loved. This will come through connecting with God and having conversations with Him about being loving.

It doesn't matter if, at first, you don't see a change. Change takes place internally before you ever see it externally. It's like a seed being planted. You don't see what is happening underground, but something is happening. Your infusion of love into a situation is like watering the seed you planted.

In time, the seed starts to grow and eventually produces the flower or fruit that you planted. Have faith in the process that planting good seed into your relationship will harvest something good if you stick with it.

Matthew 5:44 (NLT)
But I say, love your enemies! Pray for those who persecute you!

It is very hard to stay mad and choose to not love a person when you are praying for them. Particularly, when you are looking for ways to love them. This is the power of walking with God as your source of love. You can rely on Him to give you everything you need. Rely on His characteristic of being unmovable so you can stand unshakeable.

Pray for everyone you have any issues with. You can pray for the other person if there's infidelity in your relationship. You will have a hard time hating that person if you're praying for them. You can speak good things over that person and pray that their marriage is restored (if they have left their spouse for yours). Pray that God turns their heart to His truth. You may think you are powerless, and that you can't change things, but that is not the truth. Your prayers are powerful and God hears your prayers. God has the power to move your spouse's heart.

You can transform generations to come if this is what you choose to do. Stepping out in love is not powerless; it is so very powerful. Only in heaven will you truly know how big your prayers and love were here on earth but believe now that they are! Take the chance to choose the most amazing life you can have. You choose love and God will take care of you. You can trust God to be everything you ever dreamed a spouse to be. And, in time, it's that choice that will allow God to transform your spouse. The kind of attitude that says, "Hey, I know best because I've been reading the Bible and I'm talking to God so you need to do this..." is not your job. Just love, keep the declarations and the prayers between you and God, and allow the Holy Spirit to turn your spouse's heart back home and then their actions will follow.

Habakkuk 2:2 (NIV)
Then the LORD replied: "Write down the revelation and make it plain on tablets so that a herald may run with it.

Keep track of the victories! You will forget all the little good things that happen, so write them down in a journal so you can look back and be reminded of God's faithfulness. If your spouse smiles at you... write it down, maybe they haven't smiled in months. It may seem tiny but it's big. It means you are going in the right direction. From small to large, write them down and let them be an encouragement on the hard days. It is on days that are tough that you can go back and realize that every day isn't going to be hard.

I will talk more about covenant in the next chapter, but for now, know that you, God and your spouse are joined together in a covenant. Therefore, looking to God as your source is something that we should all do because He is an integral part of our marriage relationship.

Ecclesiastes 4:12 (NIV)
Though one may be overpowered, two can defend themselves. A cord of three strands is not quickly broken.

Be Encouraged

(Testimony by Rebecca)

I was bound in a prison of needing my husband's approval to feel valued and loved in my life. At that time, I did not realize the tremendous amount of pressure I was putting on my husband to meet the needs that only Christ could fill. Discovering that God could be all that I needed when it came to love was life-altering. I began to carve out mornings, afternoons and minutes here and there to just be in His presence. I was just wrecked by how much love I could feel by listening to the Holy Spirit speak words of life and love to me. I often felt I couldn't get enough. It may sound odd but I became so in love with being filled by Jesus that I forgot that I was not created to be filled but to be emptied and filled again.

I couldn't hear my husband's needs during this time because I had emotionally left. God is meant to be in every part of our lives so that we can love others. Having God in the center of your marriage means He is part of your marriage with your spouse. He fills in the gaps and is also the source of love for your marriage.

God began showing me what HIS love for me looked like and how to let my heart be in the hands of Jesus so I could love my husband out of the overflow. I went from a needy, insecure wife, always in fear that I was not good enough, or loved enough, to having my love tank filled by Jesus. It was then, that I was able to use this filling by Jesus to power loving actions toward those around me. God was patient with my learning, and slowly I became my husband's partner in life. I am thankful to be on the path of learning how to love like God loves. Join me!

Walk In It

When you think about your marriage, do you think it is just you and your spouse? I challenge you to change your thinking. Imagine God, you and your spouse when it comes to the covenant of your marriage. Anytime you think something about your spouse, imagine Jesus standing right next to them. Marriage is a 3-part chord. It is not easily broken when we remember the power and love that God brings to our union.

Power

1 Corinthians 13:4–8a (NIV)

Love is patient, love is kind. It does not envy, it does not boast, it is not proud. It is not rude, it is not self-seeking, it is not easily angered, it keeps no record of wrongs. Love does not delight in evil but rejoices with the truth. It always protects, always trusts, always hopes, always perseveres. Love never fails ...

Some Things to Think About

1. Let your God-given imagination help you on this
    challenge. Now that you know the source of love in
    your marriage is God, what is one area of need you
    can remove from your spouse? Imagine picking
    that load up off of your spouse and handing it to
    Jesus. Write down what Jesus is handing you
    back. Treasure it and continue to imagine this
    exchange when neediness comes in to create
    imbalance in your marriage.

_____

_____

_____

_____

_____

_____

_____

_____

_____

_____

_____

_____

_____

_____

_____

2. Write a prayer for your spouse to be filled with the love that only God can provide. Pray that this love becomes the source for them to love you and the rest of your family. Remember: We walk by faith, not by sight. Let your imagination be an encouragement not a discouragement when it comes to how quickly things can turn around in your relationship. Battles are only lost when we declare them lost. Have faith that God brings what is in Heaven to Earth, and your marriage will reflect it over time.

_____

_____

_____

_____

_____

_____

_____

_____

_____

_____

_____

_____

_____

_____

_____

_____

_____

_____

7

It's All in the Covenant

Jeremiah 31:31-34(NLT)
"The day is coming," says the LORD, "when I will make a new covenant with the people of Israel and Judah. ³² This covenant will not be like the one I made with their ancestors when I took them by the hand and brought them out of the land of Egypt. They broke that covenant, though I loved them as a husband loves his wife," says the LORD.
"But this is the new covenant I will make with the people of Israel after those days," says the LORD. "I will put my instructions deep within them, and I will write them on their hearts. I will be their God, and they will be my people. ³⁴ And they will not need to teach their neighbors, nor will they need to teach their relatives, saying, 'You should know the LORD.' For everyone, from the least to the greatest, will know me already," says the LORD. "And I will forgive their wickedness, and I will never again remember their sins."

The wrong actions or sin you committed in the past does not make up who you are. It is God's plan for you, and the goodness and gifts that He plants inside of you that make up the true you. The same is true with your marriage. It's not the sin you committed or the sin your spouse committed that makes your marriage your marriage. It is the covenant God makes with you when you get married that makes your marriage a marriage. God created marriage and it is in the power of the covenant that holds the power to restore it.

So what is a covenant? First, let us look at another word that a lot of people define their marriage by and that is a contract. The definition of a contract according to Miriam-Webster's dictionary is "a binding agreement between two or more persons or parties especially one that is legally enforceable." This seems kind of dry for the most beautiful and important decision one could ever make in their life. There's not much love or power in that definition. This is not how God intended marriage to be.

It says in *Genesis 2:18,21-24 (NIV)*
The Lord God said, 'It is not good for the man to be alone. I will make a helper suitable for him.'...and while he was sleeping he took one of the man's ribs and closed up the place with the flesh. Then the Lord God made a woman from the rib He had taken out of the man, and He brought her to the man. The man said, 'This is now bone of my bones and flesh of my flesh; she shall be called 'woman' for she was taken out of man.' For this reason a man will leave his father and mother and be united to his wife and they will become one flesh.

What a beautiful visual. United! One flesh! This sounds like what marriage should be. So let's look at the word covenant. This is a very popular word in the Bible. In fact, the Bible is divided into two parts because of covenant. There is the old covenant, which is the Old Testament, and there is the new covenant, which is the New Testament. We live in the day and age of new covenant, and I am so very, very glad to be there. New covenant has such grace and power and forgiveness in it that I am so glad I was chosen to be in this time and age. I found an absolutely beautiful definition of new covenant. I believe this will be a huge clue as to what God intends marriage to be.

According to Miriam-Webster's dictionary, "new covenant" is defined as "a promise of redemption by God to people as individuals rather than as a nation and on the basis of God's grace rather than rather than a person's adherence to the law." (Christ is the mediator of a new covenant. – Interpreters Bible)

Hello! Promise and redemption to individuals, not based on the law! These words all stand out to me. This is awesome news! A covenant is something created by God. It is a promise. In marriage, it is a promise to live united and as one flesh. It's something beautiful and worth fighting for and something that can last forever because it is joined, created and done in the presence of the one, eternal God. Whether you and your spouse were or are Christians does not matter. You were each created by God and are still of God. Don't say, "Well, my spouse is not a Christian." or "I was not a Christian at the time of our marriage, therefore, I can dispose of this marriage because it's not perfect." God created marriage therefore it is still a covenant before God. Because God is omnipresent, He is always everywhere. Jesus Christ is the mediator; He is the in-between in your marriage. He is the connection point for us and God. He is the one that tore the veil that was hiding us from the true view of the Kingdom of God. Therefore, Christ is in the midst of your marriage. Whether you acknowledge Him or not, He is still there and ready to bring power, redemption and healing because that is how He created it to be. No creator creates things and then just decides only part of the things that He created should succeed. He wants all marriages to succeed, but without the vision of the Creator, it will be hard to have the most successful marriage that God wants you to have.

I want you to take a chance with me, as I write this scripture from the Song of Solomon, read it with the perspective of the Kingdom of God and the thought that your Creator wants you to have this type of love between you and Him, and you and your spouse. I spoke in previous chapters about this lens of the Kingdom and renewing your mind and making that your truth. Make this your truth.

Song of Solomon 8:6 (NIV)

Place me like a seal over your heart, like a seal on your arm; for love is as strong as death, it's jealousy unyielding as the grave. It burns like blazing fire, like a mighty flame.

So how do we get to this beautiful mighty flame of love? Hopefully, you're beginning to see that you have to believe that this is your truth. These are not just words from some random book. These are words from the Bible. In the Bible, it even says that it is a living word. Things that are living have power and the ability to change situations. And because these are words from God, they have the ability to change not only your natural world but your supernatural world.

Hebrews 4:12 *(NIV)*
For the word of God is alive and active. Sharper than any double-edged sword, it penetrates even to dividing soul and spirit, joints and marrow; it judges the thoughts and attitudes of the heart.

I made a point to fill my book with powerful words from the Bible. I challenge you to go back through it again and pick out your favorite scriptures. Ones that speak to you and say, "Yes, this is how I want to have a relationship with God and my spouse!" Write them down and make them into declarations to speak over your life and your spouse.

Let's say you really like,

Ecclesiastes 4:9-12 *(NIV)*
Two are better than one,
because they have a good return for their labor:
If either of them falls down,
one can help the other up.

You could declare that you and your spouse work together well and you have good return for your labor, and if either of you fall down the other one has the heart to help the other one up.

This can be done with any scripture. Make it in plain words. It doesn't have to be fancy. Just say, "Yes, I want my spouse to love me like a blazing fire, like a mighty flame and I want to have that love for my spouse and for God so that I am continually being a supply of love for my spouse." It is as simple as is that. Speak it! "Yes, my spouse has this love! I have this love!" Declare it daily, hourly. Whatever it takes for you to be convinced it is your truth.

If anyone asked you why you believe God will restore your marriage, get to the place where it doesn't take any thought to answer them... it just flows out of you. "This is my truth... and I believe it because the Word of God says it and there's power in the Word of God."

It takes time for situations around us to transform to reflect the truth of God's Word. It first starts with you. Whether it takes two weeks, one year, or 20 years, if you truly believe that this is for you, that God has your back, you can rely on Him, then you will have peace. You will be able to do it! You can get there! The more peace and truth you have about it, the more powerfully you will walk through this time.

Spend time conversing with the Holy Spirit. Know that He wants good things for you and wants your marriage to be restored.

God is working on your behalf. You do not need to change your spouse. You need to believe, and do the things God reveals to you to show love to your spouse. It is not about formulas. Yes, there are practical ways and good advice that can be followed to help you in having a restored marriage. I have tried to impart the ways that spoke the most to me. If you walk in love and you are transformed by the love of our Father God, you will be able to treat your spouse the way God created you to treat them.

It's your choice. You can choose to believe. You can choose to have whatever situation you are in right now work together for good because you love God and you are called according to His purposes. He can redeem wherever you are at. The most awesome thing about God is He makes it better than it was even before you thought you had any problems.

May it be for you here on Earth as it is in Heaven, because it is yours to have!

__Mark 10:6-9__(NLT)
But 'God made them male and female' from the beginning of creation. 'This explains why a man leaves his father and mother and is joined to his wife, and the two are united into one.' Since they are no longer two but one, let no one split apart what God has joined together.

ABOUT THE AUTHOR

Sharon lives in Melbourne, Florida with her amazing husband of 21 years, Neil, and 3 active and awesome boys, Nathan, Joshua and Bryan. She is a stay-at-home mom, and homeschools her 3 children. Sharon continues to hold her license as an architect but instead of building structures she believes God is calling her to build up marriages.

www.ingramcontent.com/pod-product-compliance
Lightning Source LLC
Chambersburg PA
CBHW060033050426
42448CB00012B/2986